SHAKE, RIDDLE and ROLL

LORI M.

San

 Sterling Publishing Co., Inc. New York

Library of Congress Cataloging-in-Publication Data

Fox, Lori Miller.
    Shake, riddle, and roll / Lori Miller Fox : pictures by Sanford
Hoffman.
        p.   cm.
    Summary: An illustrated collection of more than 500 riddles on such
subjects as movies, school, sports, and music.
    ISBN 0-8069-7252-1.—ISBN 0-8069-7253-X (lib. bdg.)
    1. Riddles, Juvenile. [1. Riddles.] I. Hoffman, Sanford, Ill.
II. Title.
PN6371.5.F7   1990   89-26235
818'.5402—dc20   CIP
                                                                      AC

ISBN 0-8069-7252-1 (hard)
      0-8069-7253-X (lib. bdg.)
      0-8069-7251-3 (paperback)

Copyright © 1990 Lori Miller Fox
Published by Sterling Publishing Co., Inc.
387 Park Avenue South, New York, N.Y. 10016
Distributed in Canada by Sterling Publishing
% Canadian Manda Group, P.O. Box 920, Station U
Toronto, Ontario, Canada M8Z 5P9
Distributed in Great Britain and Europe by Cassell PLC
Artillery House, Artillery Row, London SW1P 1RT, England
Distributed in Australia by Capricorn Ltd.
P.O. Box 665, Lane Cove, NSW 2066
Manufactured in the United States of America

CONTENTS

To my father,
because I love to see him smile

• 1 •
SCARY TALES & FAIRY TALES

What do you call a superhero with no personality?
A superzero.

What superhero makes the best sandwiches?
Wonder Bread Woman.

What superhero checks out books?
Conan the Librarian.

What superhero cuts and blow-dries hair?
Conan the Barber.

What did Jack the Giant name his poodle?
Fifi Fie Fo Fum.

What two-ton animal went to the ball and lost
her glass slipper?
Cinderella-phant.

How did the fairy godmother get to the 95th
floor?
She took the Cinderella-vator.

What is an elephant's favorite fairy tale?
"The Princess and the Peanut."

THE FAIRIEST OF THEM ALL

What do guests ring when they get to Peter Pan's front door?
The Tinkerbell.

What does Tinkerbell take across the river?
A fairyboat (ferryboat).

What does Tinkerbell use to fry eggs?
A Peter Pan.

Who is the smelliest fairy?
Stinkerbell.

Where does every dog have a happy ending?
In a furry tail (fairy tale).

Who sews happily ever after?
A fairy tailor (tale-r).

Who is the sweetest bear ghost?
Winnie-the-Boo.

What is the Frog Prince's favorite year?
Leap year.

What fairy tale tells about crime in the Deep
South?
"Alabama and the 40 Thieves."

What sheep got involved with 40 thieves?
Ali Baa Baa.

What did Ali Baba wear so that no one would
see him in the desert?
Camel-flage (camouflage).

What camel couldn't all the king's horses and
all the king's men put back together again?
Humpy Dumpy.

What tree writes rhyming children's books?
Dr. Spruce (Seuss).

BE-WERE!

Who gets lost on every full moon?
A "where-am-I?" wolf.

Who becomes hairy, fierce and odd every full moon?
A weirdwolf.

Who becomes hairy and fierce and wears jockey shorts every full moon?
An underwearwolf.

When does Big Foot step down hard?
In a feet (fit) of anger.

Where do gnomes pay to cross bridges?
At troll booths.

What did Dr. Watson tell E.T.?
"Phone Holmes."

WIZFUL THINKING

Why was Dorothy limping in Oz?
Because she stubbed her Toto.

What hotel does Dorothy's friend the Lion always check into?
Coward (Howard) Johnson's.

Why didn't Dorothy's friend the Scarecrow spend his allowance before going to Oz?
He was saving for a brainy day.

What famous dog did Dorothy find all rusted in Munchkinland?
Rin Tin Tinman.

What piece of jewelry does the Wicked Witch of the West wear when she casts spells?
Her charm bracelet.

What did Tom Sawyer name his fish?
Huckleberry Fins.

TOTO-LLY MAD

If Big Foot married Dorothy, what would they name their dog?
Toe-toe.

What did Dorothy name her pet frog?
Toado.

What do you get when you add up all the dogs that went to Oz?
The grand Toto (total).

Where did the Knights of the Round Table park their horses?
In the Sir Lance Lot.

Where wasn't Sir Lancelot allowed to park his horse?
In the Camelot.

Who had the greasiest gun in the Old West?
The Crisco Kid.

What creature carries the bouquet at a zombie's wedding?
The flowerghoul.

Where do extraterrestrials travel after they get married?
To a honey moon.

How often do you see a smurf Martian?
Once in a blue moon.

What flavor of soda does the Creature from the Black Lagoon like to drink?
Lemon and slime.

What does a vampire do when she likes someone?
Bats her eyelashes.

What is the Bogeyman's motto?
"Actions spook louder than words."

Who jumps over candlesticks and eats like a bird?
Jack B. Nibble (Nimble).

What's a pirate's favorite nursery rhyme?
"Baa Baa Black Beard."

Who went up a hill to fetch a pail of water and chop down a tree?
Lumberjack and Jill.

What did the landscaper say to the three little pigs?
"I'll huff and I'll puff and I'll mow your house down."

What did the Ugly Duckling sing to its mother?
"What kind of fowl (fool) am I?"

What is Jonah's motto?
"All's whale that ends whale."

• 2 •
WILD & CRAZY ANIMALS

What famous dog bakes cakes?
Betty Cocker.

What do you say when Betty Crocker comes out on the baseball field?
"Batter up!"

What is the saddest dog?
A melan-collie.

What command did the vet give the sick dog?
"Heal!"

What breed of dog loves to take naps?
A schnoozer (schnauzer).

What does a schnauzer do when it sleeps?
Schnores.

What do you call a German Shepherd with spots?
A German Leopard.

What did Elvis sing to the dog at the shelter?
"You ain't nothing but a pound dog . . ."

What did Elvis teach his dog?
To rock 'n' roll over.

What do you get when you cross a German Shepherd with a computer?
A dog whose bark is worse than his megabyte.

What mysterious creature did today's wildcat evolve from?
The missing lynx.

What kind of cat comes with building instructions?
A do-it-yourself kitty.

What does a cat say when it stubs its toe?
"Meow-ch!"

What do you get when you cross a stray cat with a crocodile?

An alley gator.

What do you get when you stick wild horses in an envelope?

A stamp-ede.

HORSING AROUND

Where do horses say "I do?"

On a bridal path.

Why did the mother horse wake up in a sweat?

She had a nightmare.

Where do horses commit crimes?

In bad "neigh"borhoods.

What did the horse say to the nagging jockey?

"Get off my back."

What does Leo the Lion do when he hears a joke?
Roars with laughter.

Where do electricians tame lions?
At a three-ring circuit.

What do chickens do when they fall in love?
Give each other a peck on the cheek.

PONY BALONEY

What do you say to a pony who claims he can fly?
"Horse feathers!"

What do you call a pony who snitches on his best friend?
A tattletail.

What do you get when you hitch a pony to a small plastic bag?
A horse and Baggie.

When does a talking pony stop talking?
When it's horse (hoarse).

What cafeteria is owned by chickens?
A roosterant.

What cuddly bear complains all the time?
Whine-y-the-Pooh.

What famous bear wrote scary stories?
Edgar Allan Pooh.

What do you get when baby bears stay out in
the cold too long?
Ice cubs.

How is a teddy bear like a person with a cold?
They both have stuffed noses.

PREHYSTERICAL CREATURES

What prehistoric animals ate in all-night restaurants?
Diner-saurs.

What prehistoric animal did everything in a hurry?
The prontosaurus.

Where did cavemen go to buy a brontosaurus?
To a dinostore.

What does a brontosaurus do when it sleeps?
Dinosnores.

What do monkeys plant in their rock gardens?
Chimpansies.

Why wouldn't the groundhog leave his hole on February 2nd?
Because he was scared of his own shadow.

Where did Porky keep his money?
In a piggy bank.

Where do Eskimos keep their hogs?
In pigloos.

What do you call a rabbit's wives?
His hare-m.

How does a shy rodent give money to charity?
Anony-mouse-ly.

What is the stupidest animal in the deer family?
A doe-doe.

What is the toughest kind of toad?
A bullyfrog.

What lizard tells little white lies?
An amfibian.

What grasshopper was born in June?
Gemini (Jiminy) Cricket.

What deadly insect spins a web behind the curtains?
A black window spider.

What do sleeping butterflies rest their heads on?
Caterpillows.

How do butterflies keep their buildings up?
With cater-pillars.

BUZZ WORDS

What insects write dictionaries?
Spelling bees.

What is the clumsiest insect?
The bumblingbee.

What bee can't stop meddling?
A buzzybody.

What did Fuzzy Wuzzy name his pet bee?
Buzzy Wuzzy.

What bird picks only the finest Colombian coffee?
  Swan (Juan) Valdez.

What bird comes with easy-to-assemble instructions?
  A para-kit (parakeet).

How do scientific birds measure water?
  In their beak-ers.

What kind of bird goes to church on Sunday?
  A bird of pray.

Where do ravens hang out?
  At the crowbar.

How do ducks think?
They pond-er.

Why are pelicans always in debt?
  Because they have such big bills.

Why do fish have such huge phone bills?
  Because once they get on the line they can't get off.

• 3 •
HURRAY FOR JOLLYWOOD

Who has orange hair and a red nose and can make it rain?
Bozo the Cloud.

What funny trio doesn't believe in Christmas?
The Three Scrooges.

What's a smurf's favorite movie?
"The Blues Brothers."

Who's a swami's favorite cartoon character?
  Yoga Bear.

What cartoon stars a wildcat with a mohawk?
  The Punk Panther.

SHOW WHAT?

What's an Eskimo's favorite game show?
  Seal of Fortune.

What's a pig's favorite game show?
  Squeal of Fortune.

What's a fish's favorite game show?
  Eel of Fortune.

What's an orange's favorite game show?
  Peel of Fortune.

What did the terrorist do on "Wheel of Fortune?"
  He Sayjack-ed a plane to Ha-Vanna.

What did the crew of the Bounty do when they threw their captain overboard?
  Waved good-Bly.

What does Judge Wapner do before taking a bath?

He disrobes.

Who settles legal disputes between hamburgers?

Judge Whopper.

What is Alan Alda's favorite vegetable?

M*A*S*H potatoes.

What did Oscar learn from living in a garbage can on Sesame Street?

The litters of the alphabet.

Who teased Jethro Bodine and Jed Clampett?
A hillbully.

TREKKING

Who was the weirdest captain of the
starship Enterprise?
Captain Quirk (Kirk).

What is used to clean the floors of the
starship Enterprise?
Spock 'n Span.

Who is the tiniest Vulcan?
Mr. Speck (Spock).

What erupted on Mr. Spock's planet?
A Vulcan-o.

What video game can you carry in your
knapsack?
Back-Pacman (Backpack man).

What short Muppet was born into an African
tribe?
Miss Pygmy.

What did Ali Baba say to Big Bird?
"Open Sesame Street."

What Sesame Street resident takes bets on horse races?
The Bookie Monster.

What Sesame Street resident skips school regularly?
The Hooky Monster.

What cartoon stars an inexperienced baseball player and a moose?
Rookie and Bullwinkle.

What do you get when you cross a tropical fruit with the host of a children's show?
Kiwi Herman.

What do you get when you cross Pee Wee Herman and a young hog?
A little piggy who runs pee wee wee all the way home.

What do comedians make when they walk through freshly fallen snow?
Laugh tracks.

What comedienne has the darkest hair?
Carol Brunette.

What does Benji eat at the movies?
Pupcorn.

What Academy Award winning actor works part-time cleaning houses?
Dusting Hoffman.

What handsome tree is a movie star heart throb?
Robert Redwood.

What movie stars Darth Vader in New York?
"The Empire State Building Strikes Back."

In what movie does Scarlett O'Hara go to Venice?
"Gondola with the Wind."

What best-selling book is about a redheaded scientist who drinks a secret potion?
"Dr. Freckle and Mr. Hyde."

What best-selling book tells about Shirley Temple drinking a secret potion?
"Dr. Jekyll and Mr. Heidi."

Who rents the dumbest movies?
A vidiot.

What does Sylvester Stallone's grandmother sit in?
A Rocky chair.

DOWN IN BEDROCK

What Irishman lives in the town of Bedrock?
Blarney Rubble.

Who always causes problems in the town of Bedrock?
Barney Trouble.

What Russian banker lives in the town of Bedrock?
Barney Ruble.

What garbage collector lives in the town of Bedrock?
Barney Rubbish.

When do Donald and Daffy Duck wake up?
At the quack of dawn.

What do you get when Mickey and Minnie Mouse stay out in the cold too long?
Mice cubes.

Why did Alvin, Simon and Theodore enter the monastery?

To become chipmonks.

What comical moose can get a strike and a spare in every game?

Bowlingwinkle.

What is an office worker's favorite sit-com?

"The Fax of Life."

How does Dumbo call his friends?

On the elephone.

What does Olive Oyl put cream cheese on?
  A Popeye (poppy) seed bagel.

What cartoon features only male heroes?
  "Misters of the Universe."

What cartoon stars She-Ra and He-Man in college?
  "Masters of the University."

What do you get when you cross a daytime drama with a talk show?
  A soap Oprah.

What is a rustproofer's favorite soap opera?
  "The Young and the Rustless."

What is an astronomer's favorite soap opera?
  "Orion's (Ryan's) Hope."

• 4 •

OUT & ABOUT

What did Lawrence of Arabia say after walking across the Sahara desert?
"Long time no sea."

What happens when Canada loses its balance?
Niagara Falls.

What happens when a pyramid falls into the ocean?
It sphinx (sinks).

Why didn't anyone get angry with the baby goat when it played a practical joke?
It was just kid-ding around.

Where do Russians get milk?
From Mos-cows.

What do you get when a cow stumbles?
Chipped beef.

Which farm animal won't drink real coffee?
De calf.

What young farm animal was an outlaw in the
Wild West?
Billy Goat the Kid.

What did one hair say to the other hair?
"It takes two to tangle."

When does a thermometer stamp its feet, cry and yell?
During a temper-ature tantrum.

What is the fastest tremor?
An earthquick.

What step goes nowhere?
A stair (stare) into space.

What does a farmer do when he likes a girl?
He tries to a-tractor (attract her).

What do scarecrows do in art school?
They draw straws.

What does Santa do on a farm?
He hoe-hoe-hoes.

When is uranium tired?
When it loses its get up and glow.

What is the silliest flower?
A daffydil.

How do you ride a flower?
Push down on its petals (pedals).

What flowers only bloom when it's light out?
Daysies.

Where do weeds stand and wait?
In dandelines.

What is an astrologer's favorite vegetable?
Capri-corn on the cob.

What is a spider's favorite vegetable?
Corn on the cob-webs.

What vegetable is green, gooey, and grows in
the Black Lagoon?
A slime-a bean.

How does Mr. Fixit put vegetables back
together?
With tomato paste.

Where does a cherry tomato sleep?
On a bed of lettuce.

How can you tell if a potato is asleep?
See if its eyes are closed.

What potato went into outer space?
Spudnik.

DOG EAT DOG FOOD

What do zombies feed their dogs?
Grave-y Train.

What do sailors feed their dogs?
Navy Train.

What do witches feed their dogs?
Kibbles 'n Bats (Bits).

What do you feed a dog that eats tiny bites now and then?
Nibbles 'n Bits.

What does Charlie Chan feed his dogs?
Puppy Chow mein.

"THIS BUD'S FOR YOU"

What did one pig say to the other pig?
"This mud's for you."

What did one cow say to the other cow?
"This cud's for you."

What did one potato farmer say to the other potato farmer?
"This spud's for you."

What did Noah say to his wife?
"This flood's for you."

What did one vampire say to the other vampire?
"This blood's for you."

What is a blizzard's motto?
"The snow must go on."

• 5 •

EAT, DRINK & BE MERRY

Who sneaks into the kitchen and eats everything?
A refriger-raider.

What kind of refrigerator does Bambi have?
A Frigideer.

What is Dustin Hoffman's favorite candy?
Tootsie rolls.

Where do they make the most dill pickles?
In Dillaware and Philadillphia.

What fast food is popular in Pennsylvania?
Pittsburgers.

What kind of shoes does bread wear?
Loafers.

Where do you mail bread?
At the toast office.

What does a monster eat for breakfast?
Ghost and jelly.

What cereal do bankers eat for breakfast?
Wheat Checks (Chex).

FAKES & FLAKES

What cereal do phoneys eat for breakfast?
Corn Fakes.

What cereal do Eskimos eat for breakfast?
Snow Flakes.

What cereal do snowmen eat for breakfast?
Frosty Flakes.

What cereal do cats eat for breakfast?
Mice Krispies.

What cereal do polar bears eat for breakfast?
Ice Krispies.

What cereal do gamblers eat for breakfast?
Dice Krispies.

What do mummies put on their toast?
Strawberry preserves.

When is a strawberry in real trouble?
When it's in a jam.

What did the melon say to his fiancee?
"I'm sorry, but I cantaloupe (can't elope) tonight, honeydew (honey, do) you want to go tomorrow?"

What do hamburgers exchange when they get married?
Onion rings.

What do you call a buffet of chicken and turkey?
A smorgasbird (smorgasbord).

What do turkeys drink wine from?
Gobble-ets.

What does Pokey chew?
Sticks of Gumby.

What did the T-bone steak say to Elvis?
"Love me tender."

What is a Hostess snack cake's favorite song?
"Twinkie, Twinkie, little star . . ."

OUT TO LUNCH

What does Superman eat for lunch?
A hero sandwich.

What does a computer operator eat for lunch?
Floppy joes.

What do downhill skiers eat for lunch?
Slope-y joes.

What does a sloppy joe become when it rains?
A soppy joe.

What does a mail carrier eat for lunch?
A bacon, letters and tomato sandwich.

Where did Adam and Eve go for lunch?
To the Garden of Eatin'.

What did Adam and Eve eat for lunch?
A Big MacIntosh.

What do the seven dwarfs sing when they cook Chinese food?
"Whistle while you wok . . ."

How does Darth Vader cook Chinese food?
In Ewoks.

What is Colonel Sanders' favorite motto?
"If at first you don't succeed, fry, fry again."

What do trick-or-treaters grill on October 31st?
Halloweenies.

WHAT DID THEY PUT ON THEIR SALADS?

What did the whale put on its salad?
Alfalfa spouts.

What did Popeye put on his salad?
Vinegar and Olive Oyl.

What did the smurf put on her salad?
Blue cheese dressing.

What did the mechanics put on their salads?
Wrench dressing.

What's the difference between a pizza and your girlfriend?
One gets taken out and one gets taken in.

What's the most scared pasta?
Fettucini Afraido (Alfredo).

What Italian dish was born between April 20th and May 20th?
Chicken Cacci-Taurus.

What famous American pioneer cooked all day long?

Davy Crockpot.

What did the Martian say to the soda pop bottle?

"Take me to your liter."

WHAT IS THEIR FAVORITE SODA?

What is a Hawaiian's favorite soda?

Diet Coc-onut.

What is a lunatic's favorite soda?

Kook-a-cola.

What is Sigmund Freud's favorite soda?

Diet Kook.

What does Luke Skywalker's Jedi-teacher drink?

Yoda pop.

What brand of hot chocolate does Donald Duck drink?

Nestle's Quack.

What did the leopard say after he finished his dinner?

"That hit the spot."

What does a male chauvinist eat at a Mexican restaurant?

Machos.

What dessert is easy to make?

A piece of cake.

What is Minnie Mouse's favorite dessert?

Cheesecake.

What does an Italian Jedi eat for dessert?

Only one cannole (Obi-wan Kenobi).

WHAT'S THEIR FAVORITE FLAVOR?

What is Bullwinkle's favorite flavor of ice cream?
Chocolate moose.

What is a miser's favorite flavor of ice cream?
Chocolate cheap.

What is Sylvester Stallone's favorite flavor of ice cream?
Rocky Road.

What is a scarecrow's favorite flavor of ice cream?
Straw-berry.

What is a smurf's favorite flavor of ice cream?
Blue-berry.

What is a tornado's favorite flavor of ice cream?
Fudge whirl.

• 6 •
ON THE HOUSE

How do you let the Munsters know you're at their front door?
Ring the buzzard.

What does the sampler in the Gingerbread House say?
"Home SWEET home."

What protects your home from intruders?
Defense (the fence).

How do chickens know who's at the front door?
They look through the peep hole.

Who does a sea serpent call when he can't get
his door open?
The loch(ness)smith.

Why did the old house see the doctor?
It was having window panes.

What sign did the real estate agent put in front
of the igloo?
"For Seal."

What do you get when you cross Orville
Reddenbacher with a snoop?
A popping Tom.

Where did the priest spend his time when he was a baby?
In a pray pen.

How do you know a clock is hungry?
It goes back for seconds.

How many sides does every building have?
Two—the inside and the outside.

What does a row of houses wear when it rains?
A neighbor-hood.

Where does a roof go to meet dates?
A shingles bar.

What's the hardest glass to wash?
Stained glass.

Why did Bruce Wayne excuse himself?
He had to go to the batroom.

TOWEL TRIVIA

What do a snake's towels say?
"Hiss" and "Hers."

What do a zombie's towels say?
"His" and "Hearse."

What do a gladiator's towels say?
"Ben-His" and "Ben-Hurs."

What do a barber's towels say?
"His" and "Hairs."

What did the nagging frog say to his wife when she made a mistake?
"I toad you so!"

What do they call people who are expert at saying they're sorry?
Make-up artists.

What riddle makes everyone laugh?
A joke-of-all-trades.

When you kill someone with kindness, what do you get charged with?
Assault and flattery.

Why did the 85-year-old grandmother have purple hair?
She was a punk rocker.

What famous painting shows a tough old lady in a rocking chair?
"Wrestler's Mother (Whistler's Mother)."

What does Santa say when his gifts misbehave?
"Toys will be toys."

What should you do when a mouse squeaks?
Oil it.

What do you call the copy of a drawing of an ox?
A Xer-ox.

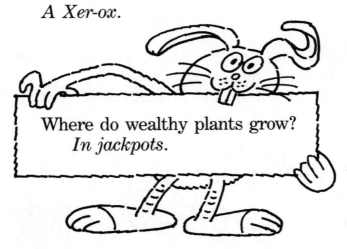

Where do wealthy plants grow?
In jackpots.

Where do coins go to bed at night?
In sleeping quarters.

When does a dimwit go to bed?
When he's nincom-pooped.

• 7 •

LOONY TUNES

What famous musical team wore cardigan sweaters and wrote songs about the people in their neighborhood?

Mr. Rogers and Hammerstein.

Why couldn't the vampire join the gravediggers' glee club?

He couldn't carry a tomb.

Why couldn't the vampire join the fisherman's glee club?

He couldn't carry a tuna.

What is a concert musician's favorite dessert?
Cello pudding.

What do musicians play in a judge's office?
Chamber music.

What rock group steals their instruments?
A band of thieves.

What's a rock star's favorite car?
A Rock 'n' Rolls-Royce.

What did the band play at the crooked politician's wedding?
"Here Comes the Bribe."

What kind of bird loves punk music?
A mo-hawk.

What kind of bird likes ballet music?
A cockatutu.

What is Benji's favorite ballet music?
"The Muttcracker Suite."

What is Kermit the Frog's favorite ballet music?
"The Nutcroaker Suite."

How do dogs dance in Oz?
On their tippy Totos.

What kind of music do leprechauns love to dance to?
Sham-rock.

What famous dancer founded Epcot Center?
Waltz Disney.

What is an English teacher's favorite dance?
The Oliver Twist.

How did a great composer describe his son?
As a chip off the old Bach.

What brand of sneaker does a great composer wear?
Ree-Bach.

When is a drum tired?
When it is beat.

What musical instrument do pastry chefs play?
The eclair-inet.

What musical instrument did the Old Woman Who Lived in a Shoe play?
The shoehorn.

What does a musician feed her cat?
Tender Fiddles (Vittles).

What do you get when Sylvester Stallone plays the guitar?
Rocky 'n' roll.

What did Rocky say when his fans were bothering him?
"I want to be Stallone (alone)."

What do you get when lightning strikes Elvis?
Shock 'n' roll.

What did they call Mozart when he received presents for playing the piano?
Gifted.

Who teaches you to play the recorder?
A tooter (tutor).

When do four dolls sing in harmony?
In a Barbie shop quartet.

What do circus performers sing at Christmas?
"Juggle bells."

What does Tarzan sing at Christmas?
"Jungle bells."

• 8 •

CLASS CLOWNING

What subject are you taking in school when you write all over a map?
Geograffiti.

What bug gets the best marks in math?
An arithme-tick.

Where do you read the most boring articles?
In a snoozepaper.

In what newspaper column did President Lincoln give advice on life and love?
Dear Abey.

Who ate frozen yogurt while discovering the New World?
Christopher Columbo.

When do students spend the most time daydreaming?
During school daze.

What area of science studies how people say they're sorry?
Anthro-apology.

What do students hate to study for?
Detests.

What test does Count Dracula study for?
A blood test.

MUMMIES FOR DUMMIES

Who was the youngest Egyptian pharaoh?
King Tot.

Who was the craziest Egyptian pharaoh?
King Nut.

What Egyptian pharaoh loved to play golf?
King Putt.

What Egyptian pharaoh had four legs and a tail?
King Mutt.

What Egyptian pharaoh played the trumpet?
King Toot.

What wildcats copy answers from other students' papers?
Cheetahs (cheaters).

Where do algebra teachers soak after a long hard day?
In the math tub.

What donuts can't pass a math test?
Flunkin' Donuts.

What do math teachers eat from?
Multiplication tables.

What do math teachers use to plow underground cornfields?
Subtractors.

What's a geometry teacher's favorite place in New York City?
Times Square.

Why did the geometry teacher comb her hair?
To get out the rec-tangles.

Where do geometry teachers go on Friday nights?
Square dancing.

What does a skunk do before it goes to school?
Puts on its stinking (thinking) cap.

What kind of school do little witches go to?
Charm school.

What do little witches learn in school?
How to spell.

What did the teacher do with the mischievous little cat?
Made it sit in the kitty-corner.

Why do skeletons go to college?
They get skullerships.

• 9 •

JOKES FOR JOCKS

What is a zombie's favorite sport?
Hearseback riding.

What is Peggy Fleming's favorite number?
The figure 8.

What do you ring to tell Arnold
Schwarzenegger you're at his front door?
The bar-bell.

What jock always arrives after the game starts?
An athlate.

What is Muhammad Ali's favorite drink?
Punch.

What kind of dog does Muhammad Ali have?
A boxer.

What do you call a great-looking female boxer?
A knockout.

What does a blue person use to ride the waves?
A smurfboard.

Where do sea serpents make holes-in-one?
In the Golf of Mexico.

What dog plays baseball?
A catcher's mutt.

What do baseball players wear in the winter?
Catcher's mittens.

What does a royal referee rule over?
His umpire.

What is Oliver Twist's favorite baseball team?
The artful Dodgers.

What does a baseball player need when he tears his pants?
The seventh inning stitch.

Why couldn't the handsome baseball player get married?
He wanted to play the field.

What did one mountain climber say to the other mountain climber when asked which mountain she should climb?
"Take your peak (pick)."

What chocolate bar does Mike Ditka eat?
Nestle's Crunch.

ON YOUR MARK—GET SET—

What did one lawn mower say to the other lawn mower at the start of the race?

"On your mark—get set—mow!"

What did one farmer say to the other farmer at the start of the race?

"On your mark—get set—hoe!"

What did one plant say to the other plant at the start of the race?

"On your mark—get set—grow!"

What did the North Wind say to the South Wind at the start of the race?

"On your mark—get set—blow!"

What did one river say to the other river at the start of the race?

"On your mark—get set—flow!"

What did one light say to the other light at the start of the race?

"On your mark—get set—glow!"

What did one artist say to the other artist at the start of the race?

"On your mark—get set—Van Gogh!"

What is a football player's favorite hobby?
Punt-by-the-numbers.

How do you make a football player laugh?
You tickle (tackle) the quarterback.

What do they put down on football fields in
outer space?
Astroturf.

What furniture roots for football players?
Chairleaders.

What do cheerleaders wave at high school
dances?
Promproms.

When do students compete to see who can clean the blackboard faster?
During an e-race.

Which person made the knot the fastest?
Neither, it was a tie.

When were the most hockey game points scored in California?
During the California Goal Rush.

Why did John McEnroe get thrown out of the tennis game?
For making such a racket.

Where do rackets sue each other?
On the tennis court.

What did Dorothy Hamill get when she got married?
A wedding rink.

• 10 •
SUMMER'S A BUMMER

How do you take pictures of a swimming pool?
With splash cubes.

What bear loves to swim?
A pool-ar bear.

Why are swimmers so patient?
Because they are used to wading (waiting) around.

What famous swimmer leaped into the pool wearing nothing but her long hair?
Lady Godiver.

What did the swimmer say to the coach?
"I'm too young to dive."

Where do swimmers sit to eat lunch?
At pool tables.

Why was the beach a winner?
Because it was shore of itself.

What constellation loves to swim in its birthday suit?
The Little Skinny Dipper.

What does Scoobby Doo like to do on vacation?
Scoobby dive.

Where do monkeys sleep when visiting their relatives?
On Ape-ri-cots.

Where does Mickey Mouse sleep when visiting his relatives?
On an ep-cot.

Where do gamblers never win a bet?
In Loss (Las) Vegas.

Where do children go to see famous cartoon characters and get sick on rides?
Dizzyland.

What vehicle burps all the time?
A hiccup (pickup) truck.

Why did the car burp?
It had gas.

What did one wheel say to the other wheel?
"It's my turn."

Where did Hiawatha drive his sports car?
On the hia-way.

DAFFY DAYS & WACKY WEEKS

When do extraterrestrials start their week?
On Moonday.

When are the most twins born?
On Twosday.

When do most people hit the jackpot in Las Vegas?
On Winsday.

When do camels drink water?
On Thirstday.

When is Colonel Sanders busiest?
On Fryday.

When do extraterrestrials like to watch cartoons?
On Saturnday and Sunday.

What do you have when a Honda Accord gets into a head-on collision?
An Accord-ion.

What happens when an expensive German car smashes into a light post?
The Mercedes Benz (bends).

What did German settlers drive in the Old West?
Covered Volkswagens.

What do you have when two ox-drawn plows collide?
An oxident.

In what newspaper column does a taxi driver give advice on life and love?
"Dear Cabby."

What kind of weed grows inside a taxi?
Cab grass.

What do you put on a young locomotive to teach it how to run?
Training wheels.

What would Santa be if he quit working and stole rides on freight trains?
A ho-ho-hobo.

How do "Wheel of Fortune" contestants travel?
In a moving Vanna.

Why won't Michael Jordan get on an airplane?
He doesn't want to be penalized for travelling.

What was the Wright brothers' motto?
"If at first you don't succeed, fly, fly again."

What book tells the story of Moby Dick's travels?
"A Whale of Two Cities."

Where do whales park?
At the Moby Dick dock.

What did the big boat say to the little boat?
"You're a ship off the old dock."

What boat has no class?
A riff raft.

What is the funniest motorcycle?
A Yamahaha.

What is the tastiest motorcycle?
A Yumaha.

 Where did the con man go on vacation?
E-gypped.

In front of what pyramid do tourists hold their noses?
The Stinx (Sphinx).

What did the pharaoh say when he wanted to keep the location of the pyramid a secret?
"Mummy's the word."

• 11 •

NOBODY'S BUSINESS

How does a bullfighter enter the ring?
Through the mata-door.

What is the first thing a prizefighter does when he gets to work?
Punches the time clock.

What does a monk wear on his head?
A priesthood.

What does the head of Sears burn in the fireplace?
Cata-logs.

Who makes sad executives feel better?
The cheerman (chairman) of the board.

What do you call a solid understanding of the steel industry?
The fundametals.

What do you give a steelworker for outstanding service?
The metal of honor.

What metal can't feel anything?
Aluminumb.

What kind of bread likes to make speeches?
Toast.

How do optometrists make toasts?
They lift their eyeglasses.

Why did the fisherman go to the doctor?
He was losing his herring (hearing).

What do orthodontists do when they like you?
Try to make a good impression.

What's the most popular learning game in banker school?
Show 'n' Teller.

What is a comedian's favorite investment?
Laughing stock.

What do you get when lightning strikes Wall Street?
A shock market.

How does a cowboy make decisions?
On the spur of the moment.

What famous cowboy film star is always complaining?
John Whine.

What cowboy produces murder mystery movies?
Wild Bill Hitchcock.

What Wild West gunfighter was actually a rabbit?
Hopalong Cassidy.

Why didn't the Australian bear get the job?
He was over-koala-fied.

What do you call R2-D2 when he takes the train to work?
A computer commuter.

What's a fortune-teller's favorite song?
"Way down upon the Swami (Swanee) River."

What mathematician always puts things off?
A calcu-later.

What did the telephone operator say when she broke up with the football player?
"Sorry, wrong number."

How does the owner of a hot dog stand wear her hair?
In a bun.

Where do cowboys get their hair cut?
In beauty saloons.

When do cowboys get married?
When they want to saddle down.

Who does a washerwoman marry?
A laundromate.

What is a baker's motto?
"Early to bread, early to rise . . ."

Why did the baker fire the bread?
He caught it loafing.

Where are the names of famous gardeners listed?
In "Hose Who."

What scientists spend their time at the mall?
Buy-ologists (biologists).

What kind of dog did the scientist get?
A laboratory retriever.

How did the man tiling the bathroom wall explain the mistakes?
Tile and error.

What is a Chinese chef's motto?
"All wok and no play . . ."

Which one of Robin Hood's Merry Men works in a greasy spoon?
Fryer (Friar) Tuck.

Why couldn't the marshland take on any more work?
Because it was already swamped.

What does a cabinetmaker get when he rips his pants?
A carpentear.

How did the wacky construction worker move the heavy silverware?
With a forklift.

What tree-cutter is found sleeping on the job?
A slumberjack.

What is a lumberjack's favorite hobby?
Stump (stamp) collecting.

Why was the angry man so stupid?
Because he gave everyone a piece of his mind.

What do mail carriers do when they're angry?
Stamp their feet.

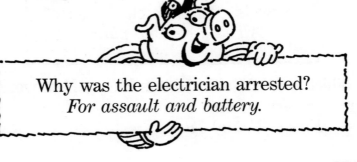

Why was the electrician arrested?
For assault and battery.

How do police officers transport hamburgers to jail?
In patty wagons.

How do sheriffs protect themselves?
They use the marshal (martial) arts.

Who gave George Jetson a parking ticket?
A meteormaid.

What do you get when you cross a detective and a crocodile?
A private investi-gator.

What private investigator attracts metal objects?
Magnet P.I.

How do federal investigators go to sleep at night?
They close their F.B. eyes.

When did the army break down?
When it was out of orders.

What happened when the soldier got lost at the art sale?
He was reported missing in auction.

What public official is full of baloney (bologna)?
The Oscar Mayor (Meyer).

How do spies send messages through the mail?
In zip code.

When did the hangman's apprentice become an executioner?
When he learned the ropes.

What did the hangman's apprentice say when he learned the ropes?
"Now I've got the hang of it!"

• 12 •
DRESSED TO KILL

What does the letter T put on when it gets dressed in the morning?

A T-shirt.

What is blue, tight-fitting and grants three wishes?

Designer jeanies (genies).

What makeup does Mary Poppins wear?

Super-calla-fraga-lipstick.

Where do you bring lipstick that's not yours?
To the Glossed and Found.

Why did the woman have three hands on one arm?
She was wearing a watch.

What does a house wear in winter?
A coat of paint.

What does a royal octopus wear in winter?
A coat of arms.

What was the lazy coat doing in the closet?
Just hanging around.

What kind of underwear do comedians wear?
Joke-y (jockey) shorts.

What do tropical fish wear on hot days?
Tank tops.

Where do lobsters hang their wet laundry?
On a claws line.

Why did Lassie's owner use Wisk?
To get out ring around the collie.

What kind of hat do you wear on your leg?
A kneecap.

What frog pioneer wore a raccoon cap?
Davy Croakett.

What department store did savage tribes shop in?
Spears & Roebuck.

What do the Merry Men of Sherwood Forest wear to keep from getting wet?
Robin hoods.

What did the little kid say after his shoes fell off?
"If at first you don't succeed, tie, tie again."

What's the hardest foot to buy a shoe for?
A square foot.

• 13 •
PARTY POOPERS

What do gamblers serve at birthday parties?
Cake and dice cream.

What does a polar bear put on a birthday cake?
Icing.

What did Mickey Mouse say to his girlfriend on her birthday?
"Minnie happy returns."

What do dragons serve with cheese at parties?
Firecrackers.

What do miners eat on picnics?
Coalslaw (coleslaw).

What is Shirley Temple's favorite game?
Heidi 'n' Seek.

What is Dr. Jekyll's favorite game?
Hyde 'n' Seek.

What is a submarine's favorite game?
Hide 'n' Sink.

BOO-BY PRIZE

What's Mr. Goofup's favorite game?
Peek-a-booboo.

What's a crybaby's favorite game?
Peek-a-boohoo.

What's a baby chick's favorite game?
Peck-a-boo.

What's a baby ghost's favorite game?
Peek-a-Boo!

What is a firefighter's favorite game?
Follow the ladder.

TICKED OFF

What's an accountant's favorite game?
Tic-tax-toe.

What's a train's favorite game?
Tic-track-toe.

What's an elephant's favorite game?
Tic-tusk-toe.

What's a magician's favorite game?
Trick-tac-toe.

What's a ballerina's favorite game?
Tic-tac-tutu.

What's the Wizard of Oz's favorite game?
Tic-tac-Toto.

What's a clock's favorite game?
Tick-tock-toe.

What's a dressmaker's favorite game?
Tic-tuck-toe.

What short dictator had the most fun?
Napoleon Bonaparty.

When do gorillas dance with roses in their teeth?
When they're doing the orangutan-go.

A PLACE LIKE THIS!

What did the diver say when he opened the ugly oyster?
"What's a nice pearl like you doing in a place like this?"

What did the chef say to the barbecue in the vacant lot?
"What's a nice grill like you doing in a place like this?"

What did Prince Charming say to the princess in the broken-down castle?
"What's a nice girl like you doing in a palace like this?"

What dance do submarine sandwiches do at parties?
The Hoagie Pokey.

What dance do the Blackhawks do?
The Hockey Pokey.

What did Tom Thumb send to Thumbelina on
February 14th?
A valentiny.

Where did Robinson Crusoe walk when he got
married?
Down the isle (aisle).

What did one tropical bird
say to the other tropical bird?
"Toucan play at that game."

What did Mervin the Magician say when he
couldn't find the rabbit he put in the hat?
"Hare today, gone tomorrow."

INDEX